Mathematics and Computing/Technology
An Inter-faculty Second Level Course

MT262 Putting Computer Systems to Work

Block III
Developing Visual Programs

Unit 4
Flexible Classes

Prepared for the Course Team by Bob Margolis

This text forms part of the Open University second-level course MT262 *Putting Computer Systems to Work*, which among other things teaches the use of Borland C++Builder 5 Standard to tackle small programming projects. (Borland C++Builder 5 Standard is copyright © 2000 Borland International (UK) Limited.)

The course software comprises the Borland C++Builder 5 Standard CD-ROM and the MT262 Templates and Libraries CD-ROM, both of which are supplied as part of the course.

This publication forms part of an Open University course. Details of this and other Open University courses can be obtained from the Course Information and Advice Centre, PO Box 724, The Open University, Milton Keynes, MK7 6ZS, United Kingdom: tel. +44 (0)1908 653231, e-mail general-enquiries@open.ac.uk

Alternatively, you may visit the Open University website at http://www.open.ac.uk where you can learn more about the wide range of courses and packs offered at all levels by The Open University.

To purchase a selection of Open University course materials, visit the webshop at www.ouw.co.uk, or contact Open University Worldwide, Michael Young Building, Walton Hall, Milton Keynes, MK7 6AA, United Kingdom, for a brochure: tel. +44 (0)1908 858785, fax +44 (0)1908 858787, e-mail ouwenq@open.ac.uk

The Open University, Walton Hall, Milton Keynes, MK7 6AA.

First published 1999. Second edition 2002.

Copyright © 2002 The Open University

All rights reserved; no part of this publication may be reproduced, stored in a retrieval system, transmitted or utilised in any form or by any means, electronic, mechanical, photocopying, recording or otherwise, without written permission from the publisher or a licence from the Copyright Licensing Agency Ltd. Details of such licences (for reprographic reproduction) may be obtained from the Copyright Licensing Agency Ltd, 90 Tottenham Court Road, London W1T 4LP.

Open University course materials may also be made available in electronic formats for use by students of the University. All rights, including copyright and related rights and database rights, in electronic course materials and their contents are owned by or licensed to The Open University, or otherwise used by The Open University as permitted by applicable law.

In using electronic course materials and their contents you agree that your use will be solely for the purposes of following an Open University course of study or otherwise as licensed by The Open University or its assigns.

Except as permitted above you undertake not to copy, store in any medium (including electronic storage or use in a website), distribute, transmit or re-transmit, broadcast, modify or show in public such electronic materials in whole or in part without the prior written consent of The Open University or in accordance with the Copyright, Designs and Patents Act 1988.

Edited, designed and typeset by The Open University, using the Open University TeX System.

Printed in the United Kingdom by Martins the Printers, Berwick-upon-Tweed

ISBN 0 7492 4440 2

Contents

Introduction	4
1 Template classes	6
2 Inheritance	16
3 Pointers	24
4 Programs and operating systems	29
4.1 Program development	29
4.2 Operating systems	32
Objectives	33
Solutions to the Exercises	34
Solutions to the Computer Activities	38
Index	40

Study guide

A recommended study pattern, based on an average overall study time, is as follows.

Material	Study time
Introduction, Section 1 (computer)	$2\frac{1}{2}$ hours
Section 2 (text)	2 hours
Section 3 (text)	1 hour
Section 4 (text)	$\frac{1}{2}$ hour

You will need your computer only in Section 1.

Sections 1, 2 and 3 develop ideas already introduced, whilst Section 4 is designed to place the Block III work in context.

Sections 3 and 4 are reading sections and contain no assessable material.

This unit makes a number of course team versions of Builder projects available. These projects are complete, so that you may compile and run them in order to compare and check your coding of the designs against those of the course team.

All the C++ *coding* in the course team project files will be the same as yours is intended to be (apart from one or two intentional exceptions). What will be different are the `#include` lines that Builder inserts automatically, as well as some of the manually inserted lines. The reason is that course team file names are different from yours, being prefixed by `CT`. The course team felt that the advantage to you of being able to *run* the course team projects outweighed the disadvantage of having to cope with these slight differences.

Introduction

The work that you have done so far has involved a large element of practical work—designing and implementing solutions to problems. There has been some discussion of why concepts such as records, functions and objects are important in this problem solving process, but the main thrust has been in the use of these concepts. It is now time to review the ideas that you have met and place them in a wider context.

This review process is not simply an academic exercise. It should lead to a better understanding of the facilities that are required to support efficient program development. These facilities should be provided by programming languages and other development tools used for creating programs. For example, the desirability of reusing code leads to the requirement for an extension of the concept of an object, as you have met it thus far. Such an extension is provided by C++ and is extremely useful. Thus, as well as the review, a new facility for practical programming will be introduced and used.

Exactly what is meant by 'efficient' may vary from problem to problem.

The practical work that you have been doing recently has, inevitably, ignored the issues that arise when developing designs and programs for embedded computer systems. As part of the overall review, these issues will be considered, because they affect some decisions about the style of programming that can be used.

The starting point for this unit is your experience of using classes and objects in MT262.

- You have worked with classes and objects designed for a particular purpose. An example is the *WarehouseType* class, used in Block II and this block.
- You have made use of the Visual Component Library to assemble user interfaces. Section 2 examines some of the underlying ideas about objects and classes that are involved in such work.

A typical object-oriented system will contain both specially-designed classes and ones from one or more libraries. Even the specially-designed classes will, as far as possible, be adaptations of existing ones. Re-inventing wheels is not a profitable use of programmers' time.

Section 1 discusses extensions to the ideas that you have already met about classes and objects. These new ideas enable code libraries to be made even more useful.

Section 2 discusses the features of objects which enable a programmer to extend the capabilities of an object which was originally written by someone else and for which the source code is not available. The most important concept underlying such extensions is 'inheritance', which has been mentioned briefly in an earlier unit. The way in which a programmer can adapt other people's objects is discussed, as is the way in which object writers can control the future use of classes that they write.

Section 3 looks at pointers more carefully than has been done so far. The need for pointers, how they are used and precautions to be taken are discussed. Not all issues concerning pointers that arise can be dealt with in this course, but enough will be done to enable you to read further if you need to.

Section 4 discusses the program development process and considers the various decisions and compromises involved. It also looks at the relationship between what the programmer writes and the operating system. This section also puts the main ideas in this block in a wider context.

1 Template classes

This section illustrates the use of classes in a standard C++ class library, and considers how a programmer can create such a class by adapting an existing non-library class (the data engine class used in *Unit 3*).

Many programs require some sort of 'undo' facility. Word-processor programs usually allow the user to undo changes made; picture-editing programs allow the user to try the effect of a change and then restore the original version if the change is not what was wanted. Providing an undo facility requires the programmer to keep track of various versions of the text, picture, or whatever is being edited. To make the facility really useful, a number of previous versions should be kept so that the user can undo several changes.

Another task with the same underlying structure is often required in programs involving graphical displays, particularly programs for drawing, for the manipulation of photographs and for computer-aided design. The user may want to zoom in to a particular area (magnify it to see more detail). Having made changes, the user may want to revert to the previous view.

In each of the examples above, information has to be saved in such a way that the most recently saved data is immediately available. The amount of data (for example, the number of versions of some text) to be saved is *not* known when the program is being designed and coded, so a fixed-size array is not really suitable for storing the information. What is needed is something that can provide the following facilities.

- The ability to store a new data item on request (whilst the program is running).
- The ability to supply the most recently stored data item.
- The ability to discard the most recently stored data item.

A data type that can provide these facilities is usually called a **stack** or, sometimes, a last-in first-out buffer (LIFO buffer). A common analogy for a stack is an open-topped box with a spring-loaded plate in the bottom, as in the following figure.

| Item 4 |
| Item 3 |
| Item 2 |
| Item 1 |

Data can be placed into the box and the spring ensures that the last item is always available at the top of the box. If the item at the top is removed, the one below it becomes the new top item. It is this analogy which is responsible for the terminology associated with stacks. Placing a new item in the stack is called **pushing**; removing the top item is called **popping**.

A first approach to providing undo facilities in a word-processor might be to design a stack to hold different versions of the text being edited. Thus, a class representing a stack of strings could be designed and implemented. Each time the user starts typing in a new position in the text, a 'new'

> Each version of the text is a single string.

current version is created and the previous current version could be pushed onto the stack. A request to undo a change in the current version would replace that version with the one stored at the top of the stack, and the version at the top of the stack could be discarded by popping.

To cope with an image editing program, exactly the same facilities would be required except that the data to be stacked would be some representation of the image.

It would be perfectly possible to develop a stack class for each type of data that might need to be stacked. However, the operations on the stacks would be essentially the same, irrespective of the data stored on the stack. Such duplication of design and coding effort is quite against the spirit of developing reusable code.

What is needed is a stack data type that has a 'parameter' (like a parameter of a function) which specifies what type of data is to be stored on the stack. With such a parameterised stack, the programmer can then declare stacks of strings, stacks of images, or whatever is required for the current task. Parameterised data types are called **generic data types**.

As far as the design stage is concerned, there is no problem. It may be assumed that the following class can be specified.

Class definition	$StackType(X)$	
Type	Identifier	Description
No result	$Push(AnX)$	Pushes item AnX of type X onto stack
X	Top	Returns item at top of stack
No result	Pop	Discards item at top of stack
Boolean	$IsEmpty$	Returns true if stack is empty, and false otherwise

There are two points to note about the table above. First, the class has four methods listed, but no data members. This is deliberate: the whole point about implementing data types as classes is that how the data is stored is unimportant; it is the methods by which the data is manipulated that are important. Second, an $IsEmpty$ method has been added to the informal description. This is advisable so that no attempt is made to Pop an empty stack. In any implementation of stacks, this action would give rise to problems similar to overrunning the boundaries of an array.

The class has data, but it is private. A programmer using the class requires no knowledge of the data itself.

Programming languages that support classes and objects vary in whether they support generic data types. C++ does provide a way of defining generic data types. Better still, from the point of view of this course, a standard library of such data types exists which includes stacks.

The following computer activity demonstrates how stacks behave and how they can be incorporated into your programs. The syntax used will be discussed after the activity.

Computer Activity 1.1

Start Builder and open the project `StackEx1.bpr` in the `Block III` folder. Run the program and experiment with pushing and popping integer values onto the stack, including trying to pop the stack when it is empty. Close the program.

Make sure that the code file for the program's main form is `StakEx1U.cpp`, and its header file `StakEx1U.h` are both open.

(a) In the header file `StakEx1U.h`, locate the `#include` statement that makes the `stack` class available and identify the *two* other statements that are associated with declaring the variable *TestStack*.

(b) In the code file `StakEx1U.cpp`, inspect the code of the two button click event handlers and hence identify the names of the methods used in the implementation of the stack class provided by the library.

Change the declaration of *TestStack* to the following.

```
stack <AnsiString> TestStack;
```

Edit the first four lines of the `Push` button event handler code so that the body begins as follows.

```
AnsiString InString;
    InString = Value->Text;
    TestStack.push(InString);
    Display->Lines->Add("Pushing " + InString + " onto stack.");
```

(c) Run the revised version of the program and check that its output is what you would expect.

[*Solution on page 38*]

The example program that you have just explored has two new items which are now discussed. The first (in the header file) is the **using namespace** statement.

```
using namespace std;
```

Modular program development and reusable code libraries bring a problem that has largely been ignored until now: possible clashes of identifiers. A programmer may `#include` a number of files to gain access to libraries and may, inadvertently, cause clashes of identifiers because someone writing a library cannot possibly ensure that there is no clash with any existing or future libraries written by others.

In a draft of the Builder files for this block, the `DataEng1` Builder unit written by the course team was named `SimpData`. One of the readers attempted the computer activities without having the course team files `SimpData.h` and `SimpData.cpp`. She obtained a puzzling series of error messages and found that the Builder installation contained a file `SimpData.h` which did something quite different from the course team version!

You have already seen one way round this problem, by using the **scope resolution operator** ::. The declaration of *TestStack* could have been made using it as follows.

> You could remove the `using namespace` statement and amend the declaration in the `StackEx1.bpr` project to try this out.

```
std::stack <int> TestStack;
```

This declaration makes it clear that it is the `stack` class as defined in the library `std` that is to be used. Placing a `using namespace` statement in program code is better if several references to items from the same library are to be used.

The full story of namespaces is quite complex but, for the purposes of this course, it is enough to regard them as an alternative to repeated use of the scope resolution operator. If the compiler does not recognise an identifier, it looks to see if a namespace statement is included. Thus, the compiler would not recognise `stack <int>` on its own, but if the statement

```
using namespace std;
```

is present, it tries again, this time looking for `std::stack <int>`, which it finds in the `std` class library. (Similar remarks apply to other class libraries.)

Namespaces are valid from wherever the `using namespace` statement occurs to the end of that file. This may lead to other files 'knowing' about the namespace, if you have `#include`d the file with the `using namespace` statement.

The second new feature is in the declaration of *TestStack*.

```
stack <int> TestStack;
```

> It is suggested that this declaration is read as '*TestStack* is a stack of integers'.

The name of the class (`stack`) is followed by the type of data that is to be stored on the stack, in this case integer data, enclosed in angle brackets. The `stack` class, used in `StackEx1U.h`, is an example of a **parameterised** or **template** class. In C++, it is usual to use the term 'template class'.

The use of a template class to implement stacks, means that a programmer can have stacks of any data type required, including programmer-defined ones. The `stack` template class can cope with creating a stack of types that were not known about when the class was written. For example, the MT262 *WarehouseType* class was not in existence when the `std` class library was written. In spite of this, if you wished, you could declare a stack of warehouses as follows.

```
std::stack <WarehouseType> WHStack;
```

The stack operations could then be used on *WHStack*. The existence of template classes greatly extends the scope for code reuse; they are the C++ implementation of generic data types.

As an exercise in using stacks, you are now asked to design and implement an 'undo' facility in the primitive text editor described in the following problem specification. Most of the editor design and coding has been done by the course team; you are asked just to implement the undo feature.

Problem Specification   Undo Editing

A partially completed text editor is to have an undo facility added. Each time the text is about to be changed by

- deleting selected text,
- cutting selected text,
- copying selected text,
- pasting text,

Deleting selected text merely discards it; cutting selected text moves it to the clipboard, for possible reuse.

the current version is to be saved to a stack first.

An Undo menu item is to be provided which should restore the most recently saved version of the text, to become the current text. The most recently saved version (in the stack) should then be discarded from the stack.

A simple text editor has been designed and partially implemented. The event handlers for deleting, cutting, copying and pasting have all been designed and coded, except for the (temporary) saving of the current text. The event handler for the Undo menu item has not been designed.

The relevant parts of the data table (written in C++ terminology) are as follows.

Type	Identifier	Description
TMemo	*Display*	Memo object to display text
AnsiString	*Display→Text*	Current text
stack(AnsiString)	*SaveStack*	Stack for saving versions of text

Design and code the additions to existing event handlers, and design and code the Undo event handler.   □

Exercise 1.1

(a) What addition is required to each of the partially completed event handlers?

(b) Express the addition as a C++ statement.

Exercise 1.2

(a) Give a top-level design for the Undo event handler.

(b) Refine the top-level design, using the terminology of the data table above.

(c) Express the refined design in C++ code.

Exercise 1.3

(a) What form will the declaration of *SaveStack* take?

(b) What will have to be added to the appropriate file to make the declaration acceptable to the compiler?

[*Solutions on page 34*]

Computer Activity 1.2

Open the project `UndoEx.bpr` in the `Block III` folder. Ensure that both the form code file `UndoExU.cpp` and the header file `UndoExU.h` are open in the Code Editor. These files contain comments indicating where you need to make additions.

Make all the additions that you have developed in the previous exercises. Run your version of the program and check that the `Undo` menu item works as expected. You should type in some text, select part of it (by clicking and dragging the cursor or by using `Shift` plus arrow keys) and then cutting, copying, pasting, and so on. You should find that the `Undo` command enables you to restore successively older versions of your text.

[*Solution on page 39*]

The computer activity that you have just done is intended only as an exercise in using stack operations, although it does illustrate the sort of actions that an 'undo' facility requires. The approach used in `UndoEx.bpr` is open to a number of problems, not least that the system might run out of resources for the stack. If a large number of versions of a large document were pushed onto the stack, much memory could be used up. In a practical program, some sort of limit would be placed on the number of changes that could be undone. It is also unlikely that the whole text would be saved; some way of saving only the changes would be used.

The stack is only one of a number of useful generic data types. One which is widely used for such purposes as sending documents to a printer is the **queue**. A (computing) queue behaves in the same way as a well-disciplined queue at a supermarket checkout: items (people) are added at the back and are removed from the front. Thus, the first item added to an empty queue is also the first to be removed. This is the reason for the alternative name for a queue: first-in first-out buffer (FIFO buffer). Many instrument-monitoring programs use queues to hold data from instruments temporarily before processing it. This is a particularly useful technique if data arrives at a variable rate: the queue can absorb temporary bursts of data to be dealt with in quieter times. The methods appropriate for a generic queue class are very similar to those for stacks.

Class definition	*QueueType(X)*	
Type	Identifier	Description
No value returned	*Push(AnX)*	Pushes item *AnX* of type *X* onto end of queue
X	*Front*	Returns item at front of queue
No value returned	*Pop*	Discards item at front of queue
Boolean	*IsEmpty*	Returns true if queue is empty, and false otherwise

The standard library C++ implementation of queues is available by adding `#include <queue.h>` and `using namespace std;` to your program. The C++ methods corresponding to those in the table are *push*, *front*, *pop* and *empty*. There are some other methods available, including one that gives access to the number of items in the queue and one to access the item at the back of the queue. These would not normally be regarded as standard operations on queues.

Like `stack`, `queue` is a class in the `std` class library.

Exercise 1.4

Give the C++ declaration of each of the following queues.

(a) *FloatQueue*, of real numbers

(b) *StringQueue*, of strings

Exercise 1.5

(a) Write a design that will remove all items from a queue called *MyQueue* without doing anything with the items removed.

(b) Code the design that you have just written.

Exercise 1.6

The following code uses a queue and a stack, both of strings. The queue has a number of strings in it; the stack is empty. Decide what the states of the stack and queue are when the code completes executing. (You may like to try tracing the code with the queue containing the two strings "one" and "two", with "one" at the front.)

```
while (!MyQueue.empty())
{
  MyStack.push(MyQueue.front());
  MyQueue.pop();
}

while (!MyStack.empty())
{
  MyQueue.push(MyStack.top());
  MyStack.pop();
}
```

[*Solutions on page 35*]

Non-library template classes

So far, the discussion has been about using template classes provided by a class library. Sooner or later, you may well want to write your own template classes and it is very little more complicated than writing non-template classes.

To illustrate the process, an adaptation of the *DataEngineType1* class used in *Unit 3* is discussed. You will be asked to do some of the implementation of the adaptation, and the complete class will be available for you to inspect. The class declaration in *Unit 3* is as follows.

```
class DataEngineType1
{
private:
   int Maximum;
   int Minimum;
   int NumberOfItems;
   int Data[50];
   int CurrentItem;
public:
   int Max(void);
   // Returns the maximum value of the data stored

   int Min(void);
   // Returns the minimum value of the data stored

   int NextItem(void);
   // Returns next data item (first use gives first data item)
   // Works as circular list, cycling round available data

   bool Init(AnsiString FileName);
   // Reads data from file
   // Returns true if all went well; returns false
   // if file does not exist (Size will return 0 in this case),
   // or if too many data items (Size returns 50)

   int Size(void);
   // Returns number of data items
};
```

This class served its purpose in *Unit 3*, which was to provide data for a graph-drawing exercise. However, the class could be made more generally useful if it were not restricted to handling integer data. It is certainly possible to write separate classes to handle **float** or other data. Since all such classes would have essentially the same code, it is more sensible to develop a template class.

A template class declaration is almost the same as for a non-template class. The format is as follows.

```
template <class X> class DataEngineType2
{
...
};
```

The extra features are the keyword **template** and the part in angle brackets, which corresponds to a parameter in a function declaration. When the class is complete, it can be used in a program by making declarations of the following form.

```
DataEngineType2 <int> IntegerEngine;
DataEngineType2 <float> FloatEngine;
```

Note that the class declaration uses `<class X>`, even though in use X will be replaced by types such as **int** and **float**, which are not classes.

To complete the class declaration, most references to `int` can now be replaced by *X*. (The type of *NumberOfItems* and of *CurrentItem* is still `int`, as is the return type of *Size*.)

```
template <class X> class DataEngineType2
{
private:
   X Maximum; // Type same as stored data
   X Minimum; // Type same as stored data
   int NumberOfItems; // Still an integer
   X Data[50]; // Array of data items
   int CurrentItem; // Index of item to be returned by NextItem
public:
   X Max(void);
   // Returns the maximum value of the data stored

   X Min(void);
   // Returns the minimum value of the data stored

   X NextItem(void);
   // Returns next data item (first use gives first data item)
   // Works as circular list, cycling round the available data

   bool Init(AnsiString FileName);
   // Reads data from file
   // Returns true if all went well; returns false
   // if file does not exist (Size will return 0 in this case),
   // or if too many data items (Size returns 50)

   int Size(void);
   // Returns number of data items
};
```

The remaining task to achieve a complete template class is to code the methods. The syntax is a little more complicated than for non-template classes. The method definition

```
int DataEngineType1::Max(void)
{
    return Maximum;
}
```

of the non-template class becomes the following. It is explained below.

```
template <class X> X DataEngineType2<X>::Max(void)
{
    return Maximum;
}
```

As well as any necessary changes to the return type (from `int` to X), all method definitions are prefixed with the phrase

`template <class X>`

and the full method name is `DataEngineType2<X>::Max` rather than just `DataEngineType2::Max`.

Exercise 1.7

Write down the C++ definitions of the methods *Min* and *Size* for the *DataEngineType2* class.

[*Solution on page 36*]

The implementation of the methods *Init* and *NextItem* will not be discussed here. However, so that you can see a complete implementation, a Builder project using the *DataEngineType2* class is provided. The project is an adaptation of the one that you worked on in *Unit 3*.

There is a slight complication in the way that template classes are actually incorporated into a project. For reasons which are beyond the scope of this course, the easiest way to declare your own template classes is to put both the declaration *and* implementation into a header file. In this example project, the class declaration and implementation is in the file `DataEng2.h`, which you are asked to *inspect* in the next computer activity. (You are strongly urged not to change the file.)

The `std` class library uses this approach of putting everything in the header file.

Computer Activity 1.3

Open the project `CTU4Ex1.bpr` in the `Block III` folder.

(a) Locate the declaration of the *DataEngine* object. What is the name of the data file being used?

   Run the project and note the data display.

(b) In `CTU4Ex1U.h`, alter the declaration of *DataEngine* to the following.

   `DataEngineType2 <float> DataEngine;`

   In `CTU4Ex1U.cpp`, change the line using *Init* to the following.

   `if (DataEngine.Init("U4FData.dat"));`

   Run the revised project.

(c) Open the file `DataEng2.h` (using `Any file (*.*)` in the drop-down list), and check the features of the template class definition discussed above. (Do not be tempted to change this file.)

[*Solution on page 39*]

This concludes the brief look at generic data types and their implementation in C++ as template classes. You have seen the basic additional ideas required to implement template classes.

Stacks and queues are amongst the most often used generic types. The support for template classes provided by C++, and the code libraries using them have greatly reduced the amount of repetitive coding required for common tasks.

2 Inheritance

The main aim of this section is to discuss some ideas (especially access control) associated with inheritance, so that you are in a position to read further and understand advice given in manuals should you need to use inheritance when writing a program outside this course.

In Block III, *Unit 2*, there was a brief introduction to the two main ways of adapting objects.

1. **Wrapping**, in which an object is included as a data item in a new object.
2. **Inheritance**, in which a descendant object is defined which has all the features of its ancestor and some additional ones.

Wrapping is, in principle, no different from using non-object data items when developing a new object. All the methods of the wrapped object are available to the programmer to use when writing methods for the new object. You have seen, and used, an example of wrapping in the solution to the Undo Editing problem in Section 1. The object representing the program window included a *Display* data item of type *TMemo* (see file `StackEx1U.h`), which is a component for displaying and editing text. (The data item is actually a pointer to a *TMemo*. Pointers are discussed in the next section.) The event handler which displayed information about stack operations included statements of the following form.

Since a variable of type `struct` is really just a restricted object (it has only **public** access), you can think of *Bins*, from the Warehouse problem, as being wrapped in an object of type *WarehouseType*.

```
Display->Lines->Add(...);
```

The situation is illustrated by the following diagram.

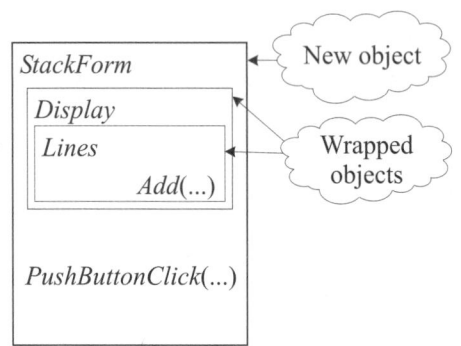

Any component dropped onto a form provides an example of wrapping.

Not only is the *TMemo* object *Display* wrapped in the form object *StackForm*, but *Display* in turn has a *Lines* object (wrapped in it) representing the lines of text. Moreover, *Lines* has an *Add* method which is used by, for example, the *PushButtonClick* method of the form.

As you have seen in *Unit 2*, the *Lines* property of *TMemo* is an object of type *TStrings*.

The important fact about wrapping that this example illustrates is that neither the *Display* object, nor the *StackForm* object know how to add text to the display area. To do this, the *Add* method of the *Lines* object must be called explicitly. At the risk of being repetitive, the *Add* method belongs to the *Lines* object, not to the memo or form in which *Lines* is wrapped.

The code generated by Builder for forms makes a great deal of use of wrapping. It is a natural choice of technique where one object (the form) must contain a number of other objects (buttons, menus, and so on).

Inheritance is also used to extend the capabilities of objects, often in conjunction with wrapping. Suppose that a programmer is starting to develop a toolkit of object types (classes) for producing simple animations, in which only translations across the screen are allowed (in particular, there are no rotations or reflections). Whatever will eventually be included in the toolkit, it is possible to identify some common features of the visual objects that will appear in the animation. Each such visual object will have a current (pixel) position on the screen, and a direction in which it is moving. The direction with which the object is moving can be specified by the horizontal and vertical distances that it moves between successive 'frames' of the animation. The following figure illustrates these ideas for a basic rectangular element with horizontal and vertical sides.

The current position would be that of some one point of the object. See the figure below.

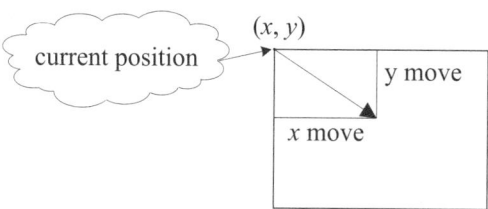

Animation objects are usually referred to as **sprites**. A basic sprite comprises a moving point and can be described by four numbers: two for position and two for movement. Methods will be needed to set and retrieve values of these four data members. So a basic sprite class declaration could be as follows.

Such methods are referred to as 'setters' and 'getters'.

Class definition	*BaseSpriteType*	
Type	Identifier	Description
private		
Integer	*XPos*	Horizontal coordinate of position
Integer	*YPos*	Vertical coordinate of position
Integer	*XMove*	Horizontal movement between frames
Integer	*YMove*	Vertical movement between frames
public		
No result	*SetPosition(X, Y)*	Sets *XPos* to *X* and *YPos* to *Y*
No result	*SetMove(X, Y)*	Sets *XMove* to *X* and *YMove* to *Y*
Integer	*GetXPos*	Returns value of *XPos*
Integer	*GetYPos*	Returns value of *YPos*
Integer	*GetXMove*	Returns value of *XMove*
Integer	*GetYMove*	Returns value of *YMove*
No value returned	*DoMove*	Updates position to implement a move

There would be no point in declaring variables of *BaseSpriteType*. The type exists only in order to have descendants. For example, if an animation requires moving circles, then *XPos* and *YPos* can be interpreted as representing the position of the centre of the circle, and a further data member, *Radius*, would be needed to define circular sprites.

If an animation requires moving squares (with horizontal and vertical sides), the position could be interpreted as the top left corner of the square and the new class can be declared as follows. (Note the way in which the class *BaseSpriteType* is specified as the ancestor.)

Class definition	*SquareSpriteType* : **inherits** *BaseSpriteType*	
Type	Identifier	Description
private		
Integer	*Side*	Length of the side of the square
public		
No value returned	*SetSide(X)*	Sets *Side* to *X*
Integer	*GetSide*	Returns *Side*
No value returned	*Draw*	Draws square in current position and size

To illustrate how additional structure can be given to the inherited class, a method *Draw* has been included which, when called, would cause the square to be drawn in its current position.

Programming languages differ somewhat in how they indicate that a new class inherits from an existing one. The important feature of inheritance is that everything declared *public* in the ancestor (here *BaseSpriteType*) is automatically available in the descendant (here *SquareSpriteType*). Thus, if *Square1* is of type *SquareSpriteType*, then it is perfectly correct to use the statement

```
Square1.SetPosition(50, 80);
```

to set the position of *Square1*, even though *SetPosition* is a method of *BaseSpriteType* and not of *SquareSpriteType*. Thus, in general,

> (public) methods of an ancestor become (public) methods of any of its descendants.

Contrast this with wrapping: methods of a wrapped object do *not* become methods of the container object.

Private methods of an ancestor are accessible to a descendant only via the ancestor's public methods.

The following figure summarises the situation.

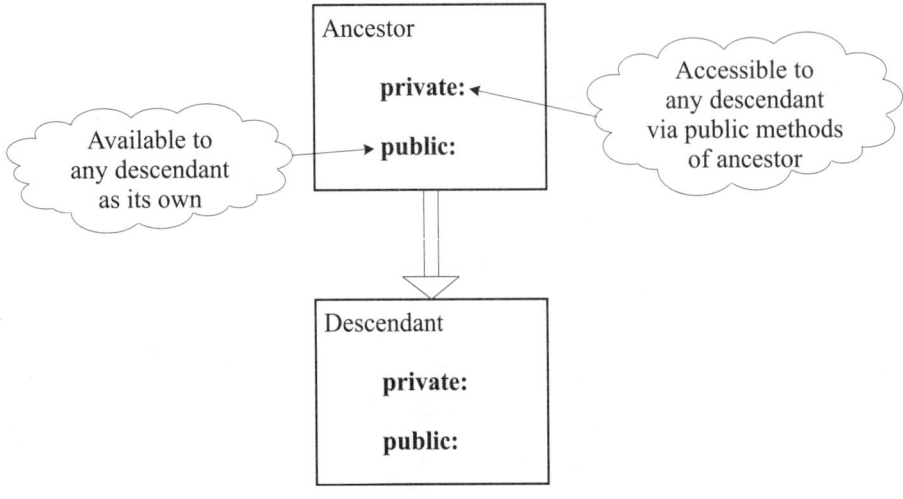

Exercise 2.1

Give a class definition for a *DiscSpriteType* class, inherited from *BaseSpriteType*, to represent a circular animation sprite.

[*Solution on page 36*]

The two descendants of *BaseSpriteType* that have been declared raise an important point. A programmer using these descendant types should probably not be permitted to access some of the methods of the ancestor type directly. For example, the ancestor's (public) *SetPosition* method should not be available to a programmer using *DiscSpriteType* because discs should be initialised by centre and radius. The desired result cannot be achieved by making *SetPosition* **private**, because that would prevent the writer of the descendant type using it at all. What is needed is an access control 'between' **private** and **public** that would allow descendant class writers access, but deny access to the outside world. In this course, that form of access control will be labelled **protected**. Anything labelled as **protected** can be used in the class itself and by the writers of descendant classes, but not by programmers merely using the class or its descendants. An example illustrating the use of protected methods is given below.

In this paragraph and elsewhere, it is important to note the distinction between the program *writer* of a descendant class and the programmer who *makes use* of an existing descendant class in her writing.

You might like to modify the above diagram to incorporate the **protected** access specifier.

Actual programming languages differ considerably in whether or not they provide some or all of the **private**, **protected** and **public** access specifiers. The range is from languages which enforce 'all data is **private**, all methods are **public**' to those which provide all three explicitly. The flexibility of having a choice, as you do in C++, brings with it the responsibility of being careful to choose wisely.

In the remainder of this course, you will use inheritance mainly in the code that Builder generates automatically. However, you should be aware of the sort of issues raised above, so that you can consult the relevant manuals should you need to declare descendant classes in other work.

To conclude this section, the C++ implementation of inheritance will be described. The following is an example class declaration. (There is no particular use for this class, it *is* just an example.)

```
class ABaseClass
{
private:
  int Count;
  int Total;

protected:
  void Init(int InitCount, int InitTotal);
  int GetCount(void);
  void SetCount(int NewCount);
  int GetTotal(void);
  void SetTotal(int NewTotal);
};
```

This class has five methods, declared as **protected** because it is not envisaged that the class would be used directly, rather it exists so that useful descendants can be declared.

19

The implementation of this class would be fairly simple.

```
void ABaseClass::Init(int InitCount, int InitTotal)
{
  Count = InitCount;
  Total = InitTotal;
}
int ABaseClass::GetCount(void)
{
  return Count;
}
void ABaseClass::SetCount(int NewCount)
{
  Count = NewCount;
}
int ABaseClass::GetTotal(void)
{
  return Total;
}
void ABaseClass::SetTotal(int NewTotal)
{
  Total = NewTotal;
}
```

The next declaration is of a class, *ANewClass*, descended from *ABaseClass* which is adapted for some (unspecified) purpose in which the ability to initialise data and obtain the *Count* value is required, together with the ability to increase the count by one.

```
class ANewClass : public ABaseClass
{
public:
  void Init(int InitCount, int InitTotal);
  int GetCount(void);
  void IncrementCount(void);
};
```

The line

```
class ANewClass : public ABaseClass
```

is the way C++ indicates inheritance. The new class name is followed by a colon and the ancestor class name. The **public** specifier here has the effect of preserving the status of data and methods in the ancestor. Without it (which is equivalent to explicitly writing **private**), everything inherited from the ancestor would become **private** in the new class. This is rarely useful, so the form of declaration above is the most used.

The effect of repeating the function prototypes for *Init* and *GetCount* in the **public** section is to make them available to the 'outside world'. Implementations of them are required, but all they have to do is to call the ancestor methods as follows.

```
void ANewClass::Init(int InitCount, int InitTotal)
{
  ABaseClass::Init(InitCount, InitTotal);
}
int ANewClass::GetCount(void)
{
  return ABaseClass::GetCount();
}
```

The only new implementation required is the following.

```
void ANewClass::IncrementCount(void)
{
  SetCount(GetCount() + 1);
}
```

This implementation *cannot* use *Count* directly as in

```
Count = Count + 1; // Would give compiler error
```

because *Count* is **private** to the ancestor class and is only accessible to descendants via the appropriate method.

The following exercise provides you with some practice in interpreting access levels in class declarations. (Only class declarations are given, you should assume that suitable implementations of all methods are provided somewhere.)

Exercise 2.2

Look at the following class declarations and then fill in the tables classifying the various items as **private**, **protected** or **public**.

```
class A   // A base class
{
private:
   int i;

protected:
   void SetI(int NewI);
   int GetI(void);
};

class B : public A   // A descendant class of A
{
private:
   int j;

protected:
   void SetJ(int NewJ);

public:
   int GetI(void);
   int GetJ(void);
};

class C : B   // A descendant class of B
{
private:
   int k;

public:
   void SetK(int NewK);
   int GetK(void);
};
```

class A			
item	**private**	**protected**	**public**
i *GetI* *SetI*			

class B			
item	**private**	**protected**	**public**
i *j* *GetI* *SetI* *GetJ* *SetJ*			

22

class C			
item	private	protected	public
i			
j			
k			
GetI			
SetI			
GetJ			
SetJ			
GetK			
SetK			

[*Solution on page 37*]

This has been only an introduction to the issues connected with inheritance, but should enable you to read further if necessary.

You may have found it a bit odd to define classes just so that descendants can be declared. It is actually quite a useful technique, as the sprite example earlier illustrates. If you know that a collection of classes will require data and methods in common, then it is sensible to define a common base ancestor class, even if the common features do not make up objects that would be useful in their own right.

If you investigate the hierarchy of Builder's Visual Component Library, you will find that a number of base classes exist just to provide common features. The prime example is the *TObject* class which provides all the basic features required by the operating system and which are common to all other classes. An actual instance (object) of type *TObject* would be useless for any practical purpose.

Another example is the *TCustomMemo* class. This has all the facilities required for a simple multi-line text editing box, but all methods are **protected**. The *TMemo* class does nothing new, it just redefines inherited methods as **public**. You might well wonder why both have been provided. Suppose that a particular application required a multi-line edit box with very restricted facilities (to control very closely what the user could do). If only *TMemo* was available, you could not create a descendant with fewer facilities than *TMemo* has. Given that *TCustomMemo* exists, you have the option of making **public** a selection of methods, rather than all those in *TMemo*.

A warning is in order here. The Builder Visual Component Library is a class library, but it makes use of extensions to C++ for *Windows* purposes. These are the **property** and **published** keywords. Broadly, **properties** are items that behave like data fields but may or may not actually be implemented as fields. The **published** keyword is associated with what appears in Builder's Object Inspector.

Further discussion of these C++ extensions is beyond the scope of the course. If you wish to pursue them further, the Builder Help system contains quite a lot of information. (Investigate the `Creating Custom Components` topic from `Help|C++Builder Help|Contents`.)

3 Pointers

In the programs that you wrote in Blocks I and II, the variables were declared near the beginning of each program, or function, in the form

None of the material in this *reading* section is assessable.

```
int Count; // Count can hold an integer value.
AnsiString Message; // Message can hold a string.
int X[10]; // X holds 10 integers, X[0] to X[9].
```

and so on. When you inspected code generated by Builder, the variable declarations usually took a different form. Dropping a *TButton* component onto a form and giving it the name *PushButton* would produce the following declaration.

```
TButton *PushButton;
```

This should be read as '*PushButton* is a pointer to a *TButton*'.

The asterisk indicates that what is being declared is a **pointer** to a *TButton* object, rather than the object itself. That is, *PushButton* indicates where (in memory) the button object can be found, rather than being the button itself.

At one time, a pointer was simply the address of the memory location where the object was to be stored. In small systems (e.g. embedded systems), this is still essentially true. However, in most desktop PC systems, there is no longer any direct connection between pointers and memory addresses. The operating system may well move data around in physical memory to cope with the varying needs of programs being used. Data may temporarily be moved onto the hard disk to free space for another program. Whatever a pointer actually is, it is safe to think of it exactly like you think of your address. Your address is not you; it is a way of saying where you live.

Why use pointers at all? When a program is written, the programmer does not always know exactly how much data will be involved. For example, in a word-processing program such as Word, the programmers who wrote it did not know how many separate document windows each user would want. There is a need to be able to create new objects representing document windows as the program is running. Pointers enable this to happen.

Compared with, say, a *TMemo* component (suitable for document editing), a pointer occupies very little memory. A multiple document editor could provide a large array, say, of pointers to *TMemo* objects, but only create the actual *TMemo* objects as needed.

There are other reasons. Some programs require a very large object, but only for short periods. In an environment where resources have to be shared, such as *Windows*, a well-behaved program will release resources as soon as possible. Pointers are the answer to this problem too.

When a pointer is declared, space is allocated in memory for the pointer but *not* for whatever is being pointed to. In order to acquire memory for the actual variable, the programmer has to ask for it. Having used the variable, the space that it takes up can then be reclaimed. In C++, the syntax is as follows.

```
MyLargeClassType *LargeThing;

  LargeThing = new MyLargeClassType;
  ...
  ...
  delete LargeThing;
```

The pointer declaration allocates memory only for the pointer (often about the same as for an integer). The **new** statement requests the actual memory for a *MyLargeClassType* object and sets *LargeThing* to point to the requested memory. When the object is finished with, the `delete` statement releases the memory for the object (but the pointer is still in existence). Until a pointer has been set to point to an actual object, it should not be used. Likewise, after the `delete` statement, the pointer should not be used.

Fortunately, for all the classes that you will use that are provided by Builder, allocation of memory and releasing it is quite automatic. You do not need to do anything. For pointers that you invent yourself, that is no longer true: you have to use **new** and **delete** most carefully. One of the most anti-social acts that you can commit as a programmer is to request memory using **new** and fail to release it using **delete**. What happens is that memory available to the operating system gradually 'leaks' away, and the system grinds to a halt. It is possible to commit this crime unintentionally, as the following example indicates.

```
void MemoryWasterFunction(void)
{
MyClass *MyPointer;
  MyPointer = new MyClass;
// Do nothing with it.
}
```

The function defined above causes memory to be allocated for an object of *MyClass* type, and then exits. The pointer variable is local to the function and so is inaccessible when the function finishes executing. This leaves the *MyClass* object *MyPointer* stranded with nothing pointing to it! The object exists, takes up memory, but cannot be used or even deleted. If *MyClass* objects are large, then use of this function would quickly cause noticeable memory leaks. An analogy is a housebuilder who builds large estates of houses, but then throws away all maps and references to where the estates were built! The houses are inaccessible, but precious land has been used up.

You may be relieved to know that if you run programs within the Builder environment, then all memory is reclaimed at the end of the run, even if you have forgotten something. This is not true if you run the programs that you write as free-standing applications.

Programs with memory leaks are created more often than might be wished, and not always by inexperienced programmers. Some upgrades to programs from well-known software companies have been issued to correct such leaks! Because of this, some other languages which support objects (*Smalltalk*, for example) have what are known as **garbage collectors**. Code which searches for 'stranded' objects is automatically included in programs. When stranded objects are found, their memory is reclaimed. C++ does *not* incorporate automatic garbage collection, so program writers have to take care to use **new** and **delete** correctly.

Pointers are indispensable for some purposes, but are less often used in C++ than in C. This is because C did not allow most programmer-defined types to be parameters to functions or results of functions. The only way (in C) of sending `structs`, for example, to a function was to pass a pointer to the `struct` as the parameter. C++ is much more flexible in this respect, as are many other languages, so some uses of pointers have become redundant. You will use them explicitly in this course only in code which creates new windows as a program is running. The disposal of objects created with `new` will usually be quite automatic in these cases.

In spite of the comment just made, the course team thinks that it is useful to show you how pointers play an absolutely vital role in implementing some of the ideas that you have already used. You are not expected to appreciate all the details of what follows; rather, the aim is for you to see how pointers enable some things to be achieved that cannot be done in other ways.

In Section 1, you met examples of template classes. The stack and queue template classes permit data items to be added in a way that cannot be predicted at the time that the code is written. It is not possible, therefore, to implement stacks and queues using arrays, because the size of an array has to be known in advance. Implementation has to allow variables to be created at run-time, and this means using pointers. To conclude this section, a possible implementation of a stack class will be given. It will illustrate how pointers enable the stack to grow and shrink, as required, as the program runs. You are not expected to be able to use pointers in the way described, nor to implement classes using them. It is hoped that you will appreciate that pointers do offer solutions to problems involving unpredictable amounts of data.

The stack class implementation uses a fairly simple idea: the stack will consist of a collection of records. Each record will contain the actual data item being 'stacked' *and* a pointer to the item below it in the stack. Because C++ does not allow template class `structs`, a class must be defined; the items in the stack will be objects, but these will have no methods. The declaration for these can be as follows.

```
// Stack item declaration
template <class X> class ItemType
{
//Data must be public as no methods are available.
public:
   X Data;
   ItemType <X> *Next;
};
```

As before, the symbol X is used for the data type that is to be stacked. The *ItemType* class has a variable *Data* of type X to hold the actual data and a pointer *Next* to the item below it in the stack, which will also be an *ItemType* object.

Now the actual stack type can be declared. This will need a pointer to the first data item and *Push, Pop, Top* and *IsEmpty* methods.

The declaration is as follows.

```
// Stack declaration
template <class X> class StackType
{
private:
  ItemType <X> *TopOfStack; // Pointer to first item
public:
          StackType(void); // No return type
  void Push(X NewItem);
  void Pop(void);
  X Top(void);
  bool IsEmpty(void);
};
```

It is worth noting that methods can accept parameters of type X and return values of type X, even though the actual type is not known when the code is compiled. There is one other new feature of this declaration: the method with the same name as the class, *StackType*, which does not have a return type specified. This special method is called a **constructor**. Every class has one and if you do not write one, Builder supplies a minimal default constructor, which is why you have not had to worry about them until now. This time something more than the minimum is required as some initialisation is needed for a new stack: it must be set up to be empty.

An empty stack, in this implementation, will be one for which *TopOfStack* points to nothing. The question is how to ensure that this is so. If *TopOfStack* is not given a definite value, then the random contents of the memory that it occupies may well point somewhere, even if not to anything useful. C^{++} provides the special pointer value NULL for initialising pointers. If the constructor of *StackType* contains the line

```
TopOfStack = NULL;
```

then it is guaranteed that *TopOfStack* does not point to any actual object. Better still, the stack can be tested for being empty by testing *TopOfStack* for the value NULL.

This discussion gives the following implementations for the constructor and *IsEmpty* methods. The implementations have the form discussed in Section 1 for template class method definitions.

```
// constructor - a special method
template <class X> StackType <X>::StackType(void)
{
  TopOfStack = NULL;
}

template <class X> bool StackType <X>::IsEmpty(void)
{
  return (TopOfStack == NULL); // Condition is true if TopOfStack is NULL.
}
```

Recall that the constructor method has no return type.

27

The next method (in order of difficulty) is probably *Top*, which must
return the data from the top of the stack. It is the responsibility of the
programmer who uses the code to ensure that *Top* is not called for an
empty stack. It cannot be otherwise because, at this stage, there is no way
of knowing what type X is, so no sensible default can be chosen to be
returned from an empty stack. Since *TopOfStack* is a pointer to an
ItemType, the associated data is *TopOfStack→Data*. Thus, *Top* can be
implemented as follows.

```
template <class X> X StackType <X>::Top(void)
{
  return (TopOfStack->Data);
}
```

The *Push* and *Pop* methods require rather more thought. When a new
item is to be pushed on the stack, the following steps must occur:
- a new *ItemType* variable must be requested;
- *TopOfStack* must point to the new item;
- the new item's *Next* pointer must be set to point to the old top item.

Before the push, a stack with two items would look like the following.

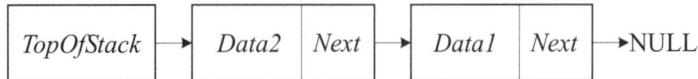

After a third item is pushed, the stack now looks as follows.

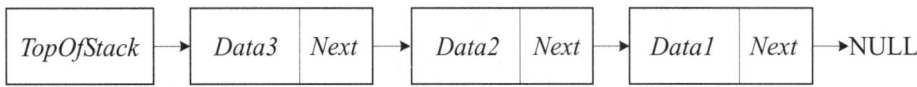

The following code will implement the *Push* method.

```
template <class X> void StackType <X>::Push(X NewItem)
{
  ItemType<X> *Temp;
  Temp = TopOfStack; // Save old top of stack.
  TopOfStack = new ItemType<X>; // Obtain new top of stack item.
  TopOfStack->Data = NewItem; // Set data of new item.
  TopOfStack->Next = Temp;
  // Set pointer of new item to point to old top item.
}
```

The situation when *Pop* is called is the exact reverse of the above. The top
of stack item must be deleted, but first the pointer to the next item must
be saved (before deletion).

```
template <class X> void StackType <X>::Pop(void)
{
  ItemType<X> *Temp;
  Temp = TopOfStack->Next;  // Save old Next pointer.
  delete TopOfStack;  // Delete top of stack item.
  TopOfStack = Temp;
  // Set top of stack to point to old second item.
}
```

The code above could form a working stack class but, in practice, that is not how the std library approaches the problem. It uses a versatile common ancestor class for stacks, queues, lists and other forms of data where the size cannot be predicted in advance. By careful use of inheritance and the control afforded by **protected** and **public**, descendants such as stacks can be given exactly the right methods.

This discussion has, necessarily, been rather brief, but it should have indicated to you the sort of problems for which pointers are indispensable. Even if you never write any code using pointers directly, you will certainly make use of class libraries in which they play a vital role. The existence of such libraries has reduced the amount of pointer-based programming which needs to be done.

4 Programs and operating systems

This section is a short discussion of some of the benefits and snags which arise when a high-level language (such as C++), in conjunction with a large class library, is used for developing programs. It also looks briefly at the relation between programs and operating systems.

None of the material in this *reading* section is assessable.

4.1 Program development

As mentioned briefly in *Unit 1* of Block I, every computer program is associated with two environments. There is the environment in which it is written, the **development environment**, and the environment in which it runs when it is completely developed, the **execution environment**. In the work that you have done, Builder provides a third environment as part of the development process: the **debugging environment**. This is the environment in use when you run a program that you have written from within Builder.

For your practical work, the development and execution environments have been the same, namely the *Windows* operating system. For embedded systems, it is almost impossible for these two environments to be the same. It is usual to develop such programs on, say, a computer running *Windows* with a suitable programming system (such as Builder). Once the program is finished and tested (often in a debugging environment which simulates the execution environment), it is compiled into a form suitable for the execution environment. Compiling on one system a program which is to be executed on another system is called **cross-compiling**. Virtually all development work for embedded systems involves some form of cross-compiling. When doing such development, it is essential to ensure that you do not use features of the development environment that are not available in the execution environment.

The choice of a language and approach for program development cannot be done without knowledge of the execution environment. Sometimes quite detailed knowledge is needed. There is no doubt that the development of languages that support the use of objects has enabled a fundamental shift towards proper modular development and reusable code to take place. This (welcome) development, and the earlier development of high-level languages such as Fortran, Pascal and C++, has come at a definite price. An extreme example will illustrate one aspect of the price.

In Block I, you compiled and ran a 'Hello world' console application. (There is a copy in the `Block III` folder under the name `HelloWin.bpr`.) As you may check by using the *Windows* Explorer program, the executable file `HelloWin.exe` is listed as 103KB in size. For comparison, the course team has written the same program using assembly code. The resulting executable file is `Hello.exe`, which is listed as 1KB. Theoretically, both programs will run on any computer which has MS-DOS version 2.00 or later (or its equivalent) as its operating system; neither requires *Windows*. The actual sizes, and a breakdown of how the sizes are made up, are given in the following table.

The source is in the file `Hello.asm`, if you wish to look at it.

Language	Executable file	System overhead	Program code and data
C++	104 960 bytes	1 536 bytes	103 424 bytes
Assembly code	581 bytes	512 bytes	69 bytes

This example has been chosen quite deliberately to underline that using a high-level language exacts a price in the size of program executable file that results. MS-DOS version 2.00 would run on a computer with only 128KB of memory, leaving about 45KB free for programs. The C++ 'Hello world' program would probably not run on such a system, whereas the assembly code version would.

The comparison is unfair to C++ in that the overhead from using C++ looks worst for a program that does very little. The size of a program produced with C++ grows quite slowly as the program does more, whereas an assembly code program grows more or less in proportion to the work that it does. However, it does illustrate the point that a C++ development system for programming embedded computers must be very carefully designed. Embedded computer systems frequently have very limited memory resources for code and data; one commonly used family of devices offers a maximum of 64KB of storage for code and 512 *bytes* for data. (For sound economic reasons, such families of devices have very long lives compared with processors for the desktop PC market.) Any cross-compiling process must ensure that only essential code is included in the executable file. (Ensuring that unwanted code is not included is partly the responsibility of the compiler and partly of the linker.)

The course has made much of the desirability of a modular approach to program development. There are a number of forms that this takes in practice. In the desktop PC world, with *Windows* and similar operating systems, large programs with many facilities are the norm. Builder itself is an example of this style of programming. It incorporates an editor, compiler, linker and also debugging facilities. A modern word-processing program will include the actual editing of the text, the formatting with different fonts, links to picture editors, and the ability to print the resulting document. In developing such 'monolithic' programs, the different facilities of the program will be designed and coded in separate modules, then linked to form the finished program.

There is a quite different approach which, until recently, was the norm in *Unix*-based systems (and some other operating systems). For program development, the editor, compiler, linker, etc., would each be a separate *program* in its own right. The code file would be written using an editor and the resulting file used as an input file for the compiler. The output file from the compiler would then become the input to the linker program. For document preparation, the text would be prepared with an editor (often the same one used for program development) and would contain 'commands' as well as the actual words. The file produced in this way would become the input to a document formatting program, which acted on the commands, and whose output would be sent to another program to do the printing. With this approach, each program carries out one clearly defined task and forms the basic module. (For substantial tasks, there would be a further refinement into subtasks, each in its own module.)

The '*Unix* approach' arose from a wish not to duplicate code. Any printing task uses essentially the same code which depends on the *printer*, not on the program creating the document. To include print code in all programs is wasteful. A number of tasks require that a text file be produced; it is wasteful to incorporate text editing code in every program that requires it. Until fairly recently, making common processes into separate programs was the only way of sharing such code.

Remembering how to write, compile and link a program was, originally, quite a task. In *Unix* systems, facilities were soon developed to enable common sequences of operations to be carried out automatically. For program development, a utility called *Make* was invented which automated compiling and linking programs. It used a file describing a programming project called a **makefile** and the Builder project files that you have used are descendants of *Unix* makefiles.

If you have met MS-DOS batch files, you will have experienced the general idea that was used.

In the *Windows* world, the mechanism for sharing code is different from the 'one program per task' *Unix* approach. *Windows* has what are called **dynamic link libraries**, called DLLs for short. These are libraries of ready-compiled code which programs can make use of (just as you have made use of code libraries). The difference between dynamic link libraries and, say, the `std` library is in when your program and the library are linked together.

With the `std` library, the code from the library became part of the executable file for your program when you compiled (and linked) your program within Builder. If you wrote two programs using stacks, the stack class code would be duplicated in the two programs.

With dynamic link libraries, all your program contains is a request to *Windows* to find the library, load it into memory and let your program use some functions from it. No matter how many programs are running using a particular DLL, only one copy of the code will be in memory. (*Windows* keeps track of how many programs are using the library and unloads it when no longer needed.) Actually, you have used DLLs. *Windows* itself is a collection of them. When you used file dialog boxes, you were using code that is in one of these libraries.

The DLL mechanism appears to be a good way of sharing code. In practice, there are snags. No universal text editor has emerged to be incorporated in a DLL, for example. The nearest is the multi-line edit box represented by the *TMemo* class in Builder. Another problem is that the whole of a DLL is loaded, even if only a few lines of its code are needed. When using the `std` library (with a good linker), only code actually used is incorporated in the executable file. Thus, code sharing via a DLL requires careful consideration of whether all the code in the DLL is likely to be required by most programs using it. If so, then a DLL is preferable to a code library. If not, then it may be better to allow several programs to have small amounts of duplicated code rather than to load a large DLL once.

4.2 Operating systems

With the growth in the use of desktop PCs, something more user-friendly than the console application type of user interface was needed for programs, including program development systems. Both the *Apple* operating system and, later, the *Windows* operating system grew out of pioneering work at the Palo Alto Research Center (PARC) run by the Xerox company (of photocopier fame). These operating systems are larger than *Unix* in the sense that they incorporate a greater range of services which are offered to programs. They act as a buffer between the computer hardware and programs to a much greater extent than *Unix* does. There are benefits to the large operating system approach. Programmers have to give scant attention to hardware details. In theory at least, to print a document the programmer only has to ask the operating system for a standard dialog box that asks the user which printer the document is to be sent to; once the choice has been made, the program simply sends the operating system a standard request to print a specified file. Another advantage is that most such operating systems provide code sharing facilities, similar to *Windows* DLLs, that do not require each task to be performed by a complete program.

To use a printer with *Windows*, a special code module called a *printer driver* must be available to allow *Windows* to talk to the printer hardware correctly. Such drivers are usually provided by the printer manufacturers or the operating system writers. Although a knowledgeable computer owner *could* write a driver for an unusual printer, it is rare for this to happen. In contrast, almost any printer can be attached to a *Unix* system by editing a text file that contains descriptions of the capabilities of various printers. This file is not exactly easy to understand, but a patient person with the appropriate *Unix* and printer manuals is likely to make the printer work, after a fashion, without writing any program code.

> A printer driver is a specialised form of DLL.

It seems that, in the desktop PC world at least, the 'large' operating system with windows, buttons, mice, etc., has won the battle. There are *Unix* look-alike operating systems for PCs, but they have not yet made a great impression on the market, in spite of the fact that a good one (Linux) is available essentially for free.

Where *Unix*-like operating systems are used, a graphical user interface (*X-Windows*) is now commonly available.

Objectives

After studying this unit, you should be able to:
- explain the main features of a given C++ implementation (as a template class) of a generic data type;
- with guidance, implement stacks and queues by using template classes from the C++ library std, and use methods of these classes;
- with guidance, design the definition of a (descendant) class inherited from a given base (ancestor) class;
- for a given inheritance scheme coded in C++, classify the access to data items of the classes as private, protected or public;
- recognise pointer declarations in C++ code, and appreciate the role of pointers in problems involving unpredictable amounts of data;
- appreciate the nature of the program development process and the impact of operating systems in this process;
- use and understand the use of the following terms: generic data type, parameterised or template class, class library, stack, queue, access specifier for data items of a class, base class, ancestor class, descendant class, inheritance of classes, wrapping of objects, pointer (variable), cross-compiling.

Solutions to the Exercises

Section 1

Solution 1.1

(a) Before any other action is taken, a step of the form

    1   push current version of text onto the stack

is needed.

(b) Given the data table, the required code is as follows.

    `SaveStack.push(Display->Text);`

Solution 1.2

(a) The basic idea is that the text is restored from the stack and the top stack element popped. However, a check that the stack actually contains something must be made as a precaution.

    1   **if** stack is not empty **then**
    2   restore text from top of stack
    3   pop stack
    4   **ifend**

You might also have considered disabling the `Undo` menu item if the stack is empty.

Provided that disabling the `Undo` facility was part of the initialisation, the event handler should not need to test for an empty stack to start with. Thus, a perfectly reasonable alternative design is as follows.

    1   restore text from top of stack
    2   pop stack
    3   **if** stack is now empty **then**
    4   disable `Undo` menu item
    5   **ifend**

This alternative does require an additional initialisation step: disabling `Undo` to start with. The course team version of the project uses the first design.

(b) The data table can be used to give the following refinement.

    1.1   **if** not(*SaveStack.IsEmpty*) **then**
    2.1   *Display→Text ← SaveStack.Top*
    3.1   *SaveStack.Pop*
    4   **ifend**

(c) The design codes directly; only the method names need slight changes.

```
if (!SaveStack.empty())
{
  Display->Text = SaveStack.top();
  SaveStack.pop();
}
```

The implementation names for the methods were introduced in the solution to Computer Activity 1.1.

Solution 1.3

(a) *SaveStack* is to be a stack of strings, implemented as *AnsiStrings*. Thus the declaration must be as follows.

```
stack <AnsiString> SaveStack;
```

(b) The line

```
#include <stack.h>
```

will have to be added to the file where the stack is declared, as that is where the **stack** class is declared. Following the earlier example,

```
using namespace std;
```

will make the class declaration accessible. It would also be possible to change the declaration of *SaveStack* to the following.

```
std::stack <AnsiString> SaveStack;
```

Either is perfectly acceptable. Because the examples provided with Builder use the first method, that is what the course team has used in its version of this project.

Solution 1.4

The C++ declarations are as follows.

(a)
```
queue <float> FloatQueue;
```

(b)
```
queue <AnsiString> StringQueue;
```

Solution 1.5

(a) The requirement is to pop items from the queue for as long as the queue is not empty. A possible design is as follows.

1 **loop while not**(*MyQueue.IsEmpty*)
2   *MyQueue.Pop*
3 **loopend**

(b) The design codes directly.

```
while (!MyQueue.empty())
   MyQueue.pop();
```

Solution 1.6

The first loop takes each item in turn from the front of the queue and pushes it onto the stack, then discards the item from the queue. This means that the first item in the original queue will then be at the bottom of the stack and the last at the top of the stack.

The second loop repeatedly places the top item of the stack into the (now empty) queue and discards the top stack item. The first item in the new queue will be the last one from the original queue. The last item placed in the queue (from the bottom of the stack) is the old first item.

The overall effect is to reverse the order of items in the queue.

Solution 1.7

The definition of *Min* is almost identical to that for *Max*.

```
template <class X> X DataEngineType2<X>::Min(void)
{
    return Minimum;
}
```

The return type for *Size* is still `int` because it is the number of items stored in the object.

```
template <class X> int DataEngineType2<X>::Size(void)
{
    return NumberOfItems;
}
```

Section 2

Solution 2.1

If the position, as given in the *BaseSpriteType*, is interpreted as representing the centre of the circle, the class needs a further data member, *Radius*, to describe the circle. A getter method and a setter method for *Radius* should be available. The class might also be equipped with other methods, such as the ability to draw an instance in the current position and size. The course team suggestion is as follows.

Class definition	*DiscSpriteType* : **inherits** *BaseSpriteType*	
Type	Identifier	Description
private		
Integer	*Radius*	Radius of circle
public		
No value returned	*SetRadius(R)*	Sets *Radius* to *R*
Integer	*GetRadius*	Returns *Radius*
No value returned	*Draw*	Draws circle in current position and size

Solution 2.2

The following are direct from the class declaration.

class A			
item	**private**	**protected**	**public**
i	√		
$GetI$		√	
$SetI$		√	

Because the inheritance uses **public**, nothing in the ancestor is changed directly by inheritance. However, the new placing of the $GetI$ prototype does alter its accessibility.

class B			
item	**private**	**protected**	**public**
i	√		
j	√		
$GetI$			√
$SetI$		√	
$GetJ$			√
$SetJ$		√	

The omission of **public** in the inheritance declaration means that all inherited items are **private** unless explicitly altered.

class C			
item	**private**	**protected**	**public**
i	√		
j	√		
k	√		
$GetI$	√		
$SetI$	√		
$GetJ$	√		
$SetJ$	√		
$GetK$			√
$SetK$			√

Solutions to the Computer Activities

Section 1

Solution 1.1
You should have found that the program display keeps you informed of the (correct) outcome of each attempted push or pop, including an error message when an attempt is made to pop an empty stack.

You also need to note that an empty string is a perfectly acceptable input string and may be pushed onto the stack.

There is an important distinction between an empty *stack* and a stack which contains empty *strings* (the latter is not an empty stack).

(a) The `#include` statement is the following.

```
#include <stack.h>
```

The other two statements are

```
using namespace std;
```

near the top of the header file, and

```
stack <int> TestStack;
```

in the **private** section of the class declaration for the program's form.

(b) The stack methods are *push, pop, top* and *empty*. The following table shows the relationship between the design names that have been used and the C++ implementation.

Design	Implementation
Push(...)	push(...)
Pop(...)	pop(...)
Top(...)	top(...)
IsEmpty(...)	empty(...)

The naming of the *empty* method could be misleading: it might be interpreted as a method which emptied the stack. However, that is what the standard library calls the method, so that is what has to be used.

(c) The program should work just as before, only now it is a stack of strings which is implemented.

Solution 1.2

The stack is for use by the project's main form only, so the stack declaration should be placed in the **private** section of the class declaration constructed by Builder. This is in the file UndoExU.h.

The #include and using statements required are the following

```
// Add #include and using statements here.
#include <stack.h>
using namespace std;
```

The complete event handlers are given in the project CTUndo.bpr.

The enhancement of disabling the Undo menu item when the stack is empty, as mentioned earlier, has not been implemented in the course team version of the project. If you wished to implement it, you would have to add

```
Undo1->Enabled = false;
```

Undo1 is the default name given by Builder to the menu item.

to the *OnCreate* event handler.

The *Undo1Click* event handler would then be coded as follows.

```
void __fastcall TUndoForm::Undo1Click(TObject *Sender)
{
  Display->Text = SaveStack.top();
  SaveStack.pop();
  if (SaveStack.empty()) // Check stack is now empty.
      Undo1->Enabled = false;
}
```

Solution 1.3

(a) *DataEngine* is declared in the private section of the form class definition in file CTU4Ex1U.h. The program reads and displays the integer data in the file U4IData.dat and should produce a display similar to the one on the left below.

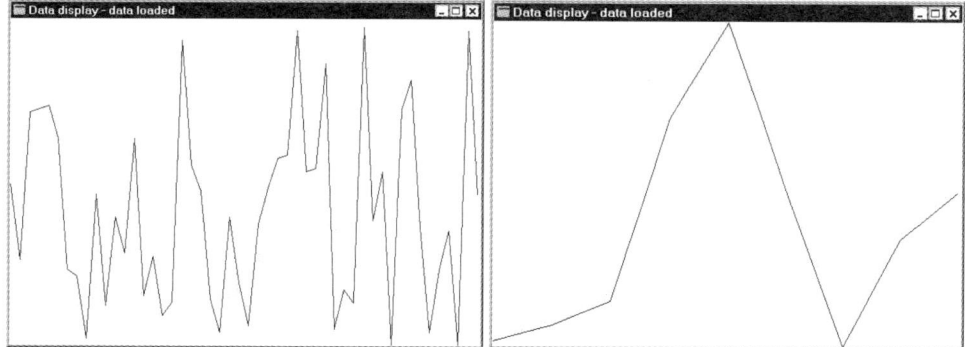

(b) The changes that you made mean that the program now reads and displays the floating point (real) data in the file U4FData.dat. The resulting display should be similar to that on the right above.

(c) There is no answer for this part.

Index

constructor 27
cross-compiling 29
debugging environment 29
delete (keyword) 25
development environment 29
DLL 31
dynamic link library 31
execution environment 29
FIFO buffer 11
garbage collector 25
generic data type 7
getter 17
inheritance 16
LIFO buffer 6
makefile 31
namespace (keyword) 8
new (keyword) 25

parameterised class 9
pointer 24
popping 6
property (keyword) 23
protected 19
published (keyword) 23
pushing 6
queue 11
scope resolution operator 9
setter 17
sprite 17
stack 6
template (keyword) 13
template class 9
using (keyword) 8
using namespace 8
wrapping 16